FINE BOTANICAL
PAINTINGS

Contemporary Botanical Works from
the Gordon-Craig Gallery

Fine Botanical Paintings

Gordon-Craig Publications

SUMMER 2000

Published by Gordon-Craig Publications
9a Trevor Place, London sw7 1LA
© 2000 all rights reserved

ISBN 0 9538557 0 8

Designed and typeset in Monotype Walbaum by Dalrymple
Printed in England by BAS Printers Ltd, Over Wallop

Front cover illustration: detail from *Paphiopedilum superbiens*
and *Calathea warscewiczii* by Pandora Sellars

Back cover illustration: *Mespilus Germanica* L. by Jenny Brasier

Foreword: Botanical Illustration and William Curtis's *Magazine*

When William Curtis launched his famous *Botanical Magazine* on 1 February 1787, little can he have realised that it would continue in an unbroken series to become the oldest botanical periodical still being published. It may well be the world's longest surviving journal in colour. Curtis's concept for his *Magazine* was to present watercolour portraits with accompanying descriptions of the many exotic plants that were entering Britain from all over the world at that time. In the preface to the first volume, Curtis tells us that his project owed its foundation to the frequent solicitations of various ladies and gentlemen and it is clear that his *Magazine* did indeed capture the interest of the wealthy gardening public.

Early on in its life Curtis had become acquainted with a young man from Abergavenny, Sydenham Edwards, and this talented illustrator subsequently provided some 1700 plates. Over two centuries later, around 12,000 plants have been illustrated by some of the most accomplished botanical artists of their day, a veritable wealth of plant illustrations that render it the most valuable reference work of its kind, as well as being aesthetically delightful.

Botanical illustration is as relevant today as it has ever been and this catalogue, which contains work by many of *Curtis's* current artists, clearly demonstrates that. It is thrilling, that there are still artists capable of works that are as finely executed as that of some of their illustrious predecessors, busy recording the precise details of a wide range of plants of interest to gardeners and botanists alike.

BRIAN MATHEW

Introduction

Wilfrid Blunt and William Stearn, the joint fathers of our 20th-century appreciation of botanical art, suggested that it was 'intent' that separated the Botanical artist from the flower painter. The intention to convey the workings of a plant in understandable and accurate detail, rather than to merely render a decorative impression.

The artists represented here are linked by this common objective and also by their desire to share their fascination and passion for plants. It is fundamental to their work that they know and understand the plant, its structures, textures and organisms as well as the rudiments of botany and the systems of plant life. However in order to become interesting to collectors and enthusiasts, botanical artists must cross the border between science and art. Embracing the freedom of one without discarding the discipline of the other. The recent retrospective catalogue of the work of Margaret Stones is aptly titled *Beauty in Truth*, again, a phrase appropriated from Blunt and Stearn. That is a good approximation of why we find this work so satisfying. The human eye knows when it is being fooled, even in such complex matters as botany. The perfectly rendered botanical painting affirms what we already know and allows us to see much more, adding to our experience of interaction with plants.

Botanical art is often slow in gestation, always at the mercy of the seasons and the sensitivities of the plants themselves. Bringing together a catalogue of the recent work of nearly forty artists has not been without its problems and I am sorry not to have been able to include some paintings that were expected. Many artists are busy for months ahead with commissions and in some cases it has been a considerable achievement to find the time to include a painting at all.

I would like to express my thanks to all those represented in this catalogue and also to some who are not, for the work included as well as for many other beautiful paintings which they have produced for the gallery. I am very proud to be able to represent the work of so many of the finest artists in this field, from all points on the globe and it is my aim to always show an unrivalled selection of their exquisite work. Many of the names represented here are well known. Other younger artists and those from overseas, less so. I hope that you will find a common thread of excellence running through the works within these pages and that it may prompt you to explore this medium more closely.

TOM GORDON CRAIG

The Plates

The following plates are accompanied by text largely contributed by the artists themselves and accordingly the lengths of the narratives vary.

All paintings are signed by the artist, though the signature is not always visible within the image area.

Measurements refer to the painted area and are given in centimetres, height before width.

Great pains have been taken to achieve accurate colour reproduction but these are inevitably subject to the limitations of the process.

GILLIAN BARLOW

Helleborus niger 'Christmas Rose'
Watercolour · 28 x 21cm

Helleborus niger is often called the Christmas Rose, although it usually flowers a little later. The flowers are pure white at first, changing to a soft green with age, as the 'petals' are actually sepals rather than petals. The fruits are attractive too, like inflated pouches clustered together in the centre of the green sepals. The word 'niger', meaning 'black', refers to the roots, which blacken when cut. Although it grows well here in semi-shaded places, it is native to lime-stone alpine areas, and is not found wild in Great Britain.

CB 2000

MARY BATES

Tropaeolum speciosum

Watercolour · 31.5 x 22.5cm

Known as the Flame Creeper or Scottish Flame
Flower, *Tropaeolum speciosum* is a hardy herbaceous
perennial climber. A native of Chile, it likes cool
moist conditions. It can be difficult to establish but,
when conditions suit, it can run riot. It has a long
flowering season and looks wonderful especially
climbing up evergreen trees or shrubs. Much work on
the Chilean flora is carried out at the Royal Botanic
Garden Edinburgh, where this species was painted as
an illustration for a projected book on Chilean plants.

MARY CHAMBERS BAUSCHELT

Phalaenopsis

Watercolour · 48 x 27cm

A *Phalaenopsis* hybrid derived from *Phalaenopsis amabilis*. The flower has a likeness to certain tropical moths and is commonly called the 'Moth Orchid'.

HENDRIEKE BERG

Hippeastrum 'Red Lion'

Watercolour · 54 x 24cm

The material, as a bulb, was found locally in Voss, Norway in the beginning of November 1999. The bulbs were planted and the best chosen for painting. The fully grown plant was painted in the first weeks of January 2000. One stem was removed to avoid an overcrowded top. The plant was painted in artificial light as there was very little daylight and the painting took two and a half weeks to complete.

Hippeastrum   'Red Lion'

LESLIE BERGE

Cycas circinalis

Watercolour · 55 × 53cm

Though Cycads have the tremendous capability of adapting to change, all 200 species are currently on the endangered species list. *Cycas circinalis* was one of the first Cycads to be named, and is an extremely variable species, belonging to a genera comprised of 30 members. The first descriptions of the plant date to 1658, and the genus was listed by Carl Linnaeus in 1753.

Cycads are distributed throughout the tropical and subtropical regions of the world, with the largest numbers existing in South Africa, South America and Australia. They were once the most dominant plant group of the Jurassic Period. The present-day *Cycas circinalis* can be found along coastal sections of South-East Asia and islands of the South Pacific.

It was a close personal friend who interested me in painting Cycads, having sent me slides several years ago. I found an enormous specimen of *Cycas circinalis* at a New England nursery and brought it home, despite its overwhelming musky odour. The plant was in the process of developing seed. The illustration depicts the female inflorescence, made up of sporophylls and developing seeds. These seeds can be poisonous.

LC Berge 2000

JENNY BRASIER

Mespilus Germanica L. · Medlar

Watercolour on vellum · 5 x 15.5cm

The medlar is a wide spreading tree. In the wild it has thorns but cultivated trees are thornless. The large hairy leaves turn a good autumn colour. Large, simple flowers, usually white, are borne singly at the end of short shoots in May and June. The fruits, two to three centimetres across, contain five seed vessels that are visible and surrounded by five alyx lobes.

The tree comes from SE Europe and Asia Minor. In countries where the fruit ripens it can be eaten off the tree. In colder countries it does not become palatable until it is half rotten, or 'bletted', when it becomes soft and brown and can be eaten with sugar and cream. If the seeds are removed it can be made into a conserve.

Mesipilus (Rosaceae): a monotypic genus related to Crataegus.

Mesipilus – from Greek mesos *half,* pilos *a ball – referring to the half ball shape of the fruits.*

Germanica: of Germany.

ANDREW BROWN

Nicotiana glauca 'Graham' · Tree Tobacco
Watercolour over traces of pencil · 61 x 36cm

A plant growing up to six metres as a lax tree. It is native to S. Bolivia and N. Argentina. It was introduced to the Mediterranean area and is now a casual of disturbed sites, waste tips and archaeological sites. This illustration was painted using a plant on a fly tip in the mountains of western Crete, and a plant growing in the ruins of a fourth century basilica in Cyprus.

APB©2000

1 cm

PAULINE DEAN

Passiflora caerulea

Watercolour · 34 x 25.5cm

The common passion flower is a native plant of
southern Brazil reaching a height of six to ten metres
and climbs with the aid of axillary tendrils. It can be
grown outdoors in Britain but requires sunshine and
a well drained soil. It is half hardy so needs a relatively sheltered position away from the worst of the
winter frosts. The flowers are about 8cm across and
are produced from June to September in the right
conditions in great profusion. These are followed by
attractive ovoid orange fruits, which are edible but
not particularly palatable.

A legend has grown up around the complex
constitution of the flowers. This tells how the Jesuits
in the 16th century, following the Conquistadors after
their victorious campaigning in South America,
wanted favourable omens for their cause as they
stepped ashore for the first time. This plant growing
near the shore was chosen and was named the Passion
Flower recalling the Passion of Jesus.

The ten sepals and petals represented the ten
faithful apostles (Judas and Doubting Thomas being
omitted), the outer corona symbolizes the many
disciples and the inner corona the Crown of Thorns.
The five stamens represented Christ's five wounds
and the three-part stigma, the nails – and the ovary,
the hammer which inflicted the wounds.

The curling tendrils were a reminder of the whips
which scourged Jesus and the five-part leaves the
clutching hands of the soldiers.

Prideau

ELVIA ESPARZA

Echinocereus polyacanthus

Watercolour · 37 × 26.5cm

This handsome cactus species occurs in numerous distinct populations throughout its geographical range, primarily in parts of the Sierra Madre Occidental, and grows exclusively on volcanic (riolitic) formations. The huge narrowly tubular flowers appear to be visited by nocturnal pollinators, most likely hawkmoths.

Elvia Esparza

ANNIE FARRER

Panicum

Watercolour · 58.5 x 40cm

Panicum is a grass genus of around 500 species
distributed throughout the tropical and subtropical
regions of the world. It inhabits a wide range of eco-
types from desert to savannah, forest and swamps. It
is important as a source of forage to animals and as a
cereal. This particular specimen was found growing
on a roadside in North Carolina. It was growing under
stress, which accounts for the red colouring in the
leaves.

GEORITA HARRIOTT

Passiflora caerulea-racemosa
Watercolour · 33 x 18cm

Passiflora caerulea-racemosa is a cultivar of
P. caerulea and *P. racemosa* and is the oldest docu-
mented *Passiflora* hybrid. It was cultivated by a Mr
Milne of Fulham, London and published by Sabine
in 1821. Its arrival was given a mixed reception with
members of the Horticultural Society declaring their
distaste at 'the growing fashion at present for the
mingling of flowers' and questioning the notion that
hybridisation would benefit either botany or horticulture. *P. caeruleo-racemosa* was the name that Sabine
gave the hybrid in 1821. This has been widely rejected
in favour of the name *P.* x *violacea* Loisel. It is a half
hardy variety which will grow well in sheltered
environments but in Britain flowers best under glass.

This specimen was painted growing in botanical
gardens of the University of Cambridge as part of a
series of eight species of passion flowers.

CHRISTINA HART-DAVIES

Carica papaya L. · Pawpaw

Watercolour · 19 x 23cm

The pawpaw has been cultivated in Central America and Brazil since pre-Columbian times and is now frequently grown throughout all tropical regions, both on small farms for the farmer's own use, and in large commercial plantations.

The short-lived tree can reach seven to ten metres, with a smooth, green, unbranched trunk showing the scars of fallen leaves. The dark green leaves, borne in a tuft at the top of the trunk, are large and long-stalked, with deeply-divided, palmately-lobed blades. The axiliary inflorescences in female trees are in short, branched clusters, while those in male trees hang in pendulous racemes. Bisexual flowers occasionally occur.

Fruits are produced throughout the year, after pollination by insects. They can weigh up to 5kg, though 1kg or less is more usual. The delicious, creamy textured flesh is free of acid and contains abundant vitamin A and C. The seeds taste like cress. The ripe fruits are eaten as a dessert or breakfast fruit, and are said to cure haemorrhoids and constipation.

The protein-splitting enzyme papain, which helps in the digestion of meat, is present in the fruit, and is gathered commercially from the sap which flows from cuts made in the skin of immature fruits. It is used medicinally in cases of weak digestion, as well as in the manufacture of chewing-gum, as a meat tenderiser, as an anti-shrinking agent in the textile industry, and many other cosmetic or industrial uses.

JENNY JOWETT

Iris ensata

Watercolour · 56 x 32cm

Since Ancient Greece, Irises have been cultivated not only for their obvious beauty but also for their magical qualities. The Greeks named the flower after Iris, messenger of the gods. According to Dioscorides both the Greeks and the Romans used the rhizomes for medicinal purposes. They were also used as a perfume for linen and are mentioned in 1480 in the wardrobe accounts of Edward IV. Several pieces of dried iris root strung on a string would be plunged into the boiling water with the clothes to assist the removal of foul odours. For centuries Europeans consumed Iris roots, or 'Orris Root', to cure bad breath among other ills. It was also given to infants for teething and its use continues in toothpaste's to the present day. On a more romantic note the iris has finally been identified by historians as the fleur-de-lis, the symbol of the rulers of France. The name deriving from fleur-de-louis, after Louis VII made it his symbol in the Crusade of 1147.

This particular iris grows well in damp conditions and on the margins of ponds and rivers.

Iris ensata   Jenny Jowett

CHRISTABEL KING

Calanthe vestita Lindl.

Pencil and Watercolour · 39 × 33cm

The Genus *Calanthe* to which this beautiful winter-flowering orchid belongs is widely distributed from South Africa through Asia to Australia. Most of its 150 or so species are terrestrial and may be either evergreen or deciduous, as the species illustrated. Within the genus the size of leaves tends to be large and the inflorescences erect and arching, sometimes several feet long. The flowers can be many shades of white, pink yellow and usually have a conspicuous lip.

   Calanthe vestita was discovered by Dr Nathaniel Wallich at Tavoy in Tenasserirm, Lower Burma in 1826 (Wallich Catalogue no. 7345) and described by John Lindley. It was not introduced into cultivation in Britain until 1848 when plants were sent to the nursery of Messrs Veitch at Exeter from Moulmein, a locality north of Tavoy in Lower Burma. Two colour forms were sent, one with white flowers and a yellow spot which was the colour form originally described and a form with a crimson spot referred to as *var. rubro-maculata* similar to the form illustrated here. The crimson spotted form was awarded a silver medal when exhibited in London in November 1848. The plant is fairly well known in cultivation as well as hybrids and other colour forms. It is not difficult to grow in a warm greenhouse, needing little or no water in the flowering season until the new leaves appear.

   This painting of a plant in the Tropical Nursery at the Royal Botanic Gardens Kew was begun in October 1999 when the inflorescence was developing and the leaves were turning brown prior to falling. The flowers were drawn in November 1999 at the beginning of flowering and when the finishing touches were made early in February 2000 the last few flowers of the inflorescence were still fresh. The flower spike is drawn life size but the leaves and pseudobulbs are drawn ¾ natural size.

Calanthe vestita Lindl.

Cult. Tropical Nursery, Royal Botanic Gardens Kew 1987-3505
Leaves & pseudobulb drawn 26/11/99, inflorescence 23/11/99

×2

×10   ×¾

×1

C H King

17th February 2000

DEBORAH LAMBKIN

Cyclamen hederifolium

Watercolour · 27 x 47.5cm

This specimen was obtained from a cold but dry and sheltered flowerbed at the foot of an old limestone wall in my parents seaside garden in Co. Dublin. *Cyclamen hederifolium*, native to the dry Mediterranean hills and woods, where it is a protected species, is hardy in our cold damp Irish climate.

Throughout Autumn this cyclamen produces delicate pink flowers, which after flowering, are pulled back to the earth, the stems spiralling like a telephone wire, when the seeds fully develop. Towards the end of the flowering season the silvery green leaves appear and last for the whole winter.

Cyclamen hederifolium can be distinguished from the other cyclamen species by the roots that grow mainly from the tops and sides of the corm. Some old cyclamen corms have been known to reach ten inches in diameter. This poisonous plant is most content to grow undisturbed and with a yearly dressing of leaf mould. They seed themselves freely and these seedlings usually flower in a few years.

JOANNA ASQUITH LANGHORNE

Ampelopsis brevipedunculata

Watercolour · 20.5 x 12cm

A vigorous climbing vine found in China, Japan and Korea. It will grow in the sun or partial shade. It climbs by means of tendrils, is extremely versatile and is suitable for covering walls, pergolas, or even iron railings. The luxuriant, hop-like, foliage is 3–5 lobed. The small flowers are rather insignificant and greenish-white in colour. This vine is notable for the brightly coloured fruits in shades of turquoise blue to bright purple. The fruits are especially striking when they contrast with the yellowing autumn leaves. They have an almost porcelain like texture. The fruits fall after all the leaves have dropped. A specimen of the vine is to be found in St Leonard's Terrace, Chelsea. The Royal Botanic Gardens at Kew have several specimens.

Joanna A Langhorne del.

POLLY MORRIS

Aeschynanthus speciosus

Watercolour · 42 x 33cm

A climbing plant from Indonesia, with tufts of bright
yellow-orange tubular flowers which are slightly
downy. Each flower lasts only a few days and they are
bird-pollinated. Extra-floral attraction exists in the
form of leaf pigmentation with stained-glass-like
optical properties when viewed against the light: the
upper part of the leaf surface is colourless and trans-
parent and only the lower surface is pigmented.

Aeschynanthus speciosus

LUCA PALERMO

Amaryllis belladonna L.

Watercolour · 52 x 40cm

This watercolour was prepared for an exhibition about the Flora of Cyprus at the Natural History Museum of Genoa in March of this year. The plant actually originates from the Cape of Good Hope, South Africa and seems to have been introduced into Europe around 1712. Its name derives from the name of a Greek nymph and the species, belladonna, means beautiful lady in Italian. That most likely came from the ancient habit of women placing a few drops of an abstract of the roots and leaves into their eyes. The effect, caused by an alkaloid in the plant, was to dilate the pupils and is much like a drug used by eye surgeons to better observe the retina.

The plant shown here is a composition of different stages, as it produces its leaves and flowers at different times. In this plate are shown the flower with several blossoms, the bulb with leaves and roots and the strange seedpods of the Amaryllis, showing the delicate rosy-pink seeds.

KATHY PICKLES

Cymbidium Orchid (unknown variety)

Watercolour · 31.5 x 21cm

Of all the orchids, cymbidiums are best suited for
outdoor culture. In their natural habitats, they grow
at the higher altitudes in the temperate zone of mid-
Asia (China, Japan) down through south-east Asia
and extending south of the equator, with a number of
species in Australia. The climatic conditions found
there are also found at sea level in the coastal regions
of California, along the coast in the Mediterranean
and in parts of New Zealand as well as South Africa.
They are more commonly grown under greenhouse
conditions in most other parts of the world. The cycle
of cool nights and warm days during the spring
months in these regions is necessary for flower spike,
bud formation. Blooming occurs from February to
May. One bloom spike may carry as many as 30
flowers, each four to six inches across. The flowers can
remain fresh and attractive for eight or more weeks.
Warmer weather in the summer enhances the growth
and development of the flower spikes for the following season. This particular specimen was painted at
the artist's home in the Orkney Islands.

BRYAN POOLE

Ficus carica · **Black Fig**
Hand Coloured Aquatint Etching · Plate size 51 x 37.5cm

The Greek Island of Cephalonia provided the reference for this popular fruiting tree. Made from two plates, the first is inked in six colours including the crimson of the fruit flesh. The second offset plate is inked in a deep purple/black, which is blended with green on the upper unripened fruits. The print is then carefully registered and re-pulled through the intaglio press. The honey dew nectar is hand coloured after the print is dry.

Bryan Poole's work is print-making in the very traditional sense. No photographic aids are used and each print is in itself an individual work. The process involves drawing the design directly onto copper with an etching needle. The plate is then immersed in acid to etch along the needle line. The etched linear drawing provides the foundation for all the other stages in the making of the plate; aquatint, spit-bite, soft ground etching and sugar lift. Final highlights are then achieved by burnishing back into the surface of the plate. The plates are then inked in four to seven colours and hand printed in an intaglio press. Hand colour is added to the dried prints.

Pachystegia insignis · Kai Koura Rock Daisy

Hand Coloured Aquatint Etching · Plate size 51 × 37.5cm

This handsome cliff dwelling shrub is simply rendered as line with two stages of aquatint etching. And the minimum of burnished highlights. It is then inked and printed in five colours. Detailed hand colouring of the flower heads is added once the print has dried and the stem colouring is achieved by mixing yellow ochre watercolour with gum arabic.

VALERIE PRICE

Ligustrum sempervirens

Watercolour · 21 x 13cm

Privet is the common name applied to plants of the family Oleaceae or olive. Privets are shrubs or small trees with opposite leaves, which are simple and entire at the margin. The flowers are small, white, and in terminal panicles.

RODELLA PURVES

Rubus fruticosus and *Rosa Canina*

Watercolour 48 x 38cm

Rubus fruticosus – The common Bramble is widespread in wooded areas and glens throughout Scotland and forms a group so puzzling to the non-specialist, differing among themselves in combinations and minute overlapping characteristics, *Rosa canina* – the Dog rose is a close relative of *Rosa rubiginosa* (the sweet briar) and often frequents the same habitat as that of *Rubus fruticosius.*

In order to obtain a degree of uniformity the two subjects used in this illustration were painted from the species growing 'wild' in the woodland garden at the Royal Botanic Garden, Edinburgh. Plant 'association' paintings are very complex, especially at the early drawing stage when composition is so important in order to achieve a good balance of colour and form within the integration of the two specimens.

Rubus fruticosus × Rosa canina.
RBG Edinburgh, October 1999

REINHILD RAISTRICK

Colchicum Dandaels

Watercolour · 27 x 15cm

Early botanists must have been puzzled by the growth pattern of this genus. The flowers emerge in early autumn, followed in spring by the large green leaves, with the seed pod in among them. So it could appear that the seed pod comes before the flower – hence one of its names *Filius ante Patrem*, son before the father. Other common names include, naked ladies or nakedboys, referring to the emergence of the flowers without foliage. They are also frequently given the incorrect name of autumn crocus.

The pink tipped white buds push their way through the soil in late August, and within a few days open into rosy – lilac flowers, with bright yellow stamens and a beautiful fragrance. This hybrid is from a Dutch selection from a firm called Zocher. E. A. Bowles, a famous gardener, noted that this was one of the few hybrids that set seeds.

Autumn flowering colchicum species occur wild in many countries in Europe, as well as the Caucasus, Iran and Turkey.

This example is from the National Collection of colchicums at Felbrigg Hall, Norfolk.

Reinhild
Raistrick. 99

KAY REES-DAVIES

Ilex aquifolium 'Argentea Marginata'

Watercolour · 43 × 30.5cm

Genus of evergreen or deciduous trees and shrubs, grown for their foliage and fruits. Mainly spherical berries, ranging in colour from red through yellow to black, are produced in autumn. Almost all plants are unisexual, and to obtain fruits on a female plant a male also needs to be grown. Fully to half hardy, all prefer well-drained soil.

Ilex aquifolium 'Argentea Marginata' (silver margined holly'), is a columnar, female tree. Height 14m, spread 5m. Young branches are green, streaked with cream. Broadly oval, spiny, dark green leaves, with wide cream margins, are shrimp pink when young. It bears an abundance of bright red berries.

Kay Rees-Davies

HIROE SASAKI

Cattleya schilleriana

Watercolour and Pencil · 13.5 x 17.5cm

This species is becoming extinct in its natural habitats. It occurs in the States of Bahia and Espírito Santo, Brazil. The petals and sepals are olive green and red, brown spotted with dark maroon. The lip is yellow and streaked with purple. It usually bears one or two flowers per inflorescence and blooms from late spring to summer (Southern hemisphere). The flower size is between seven and ten centimetres.

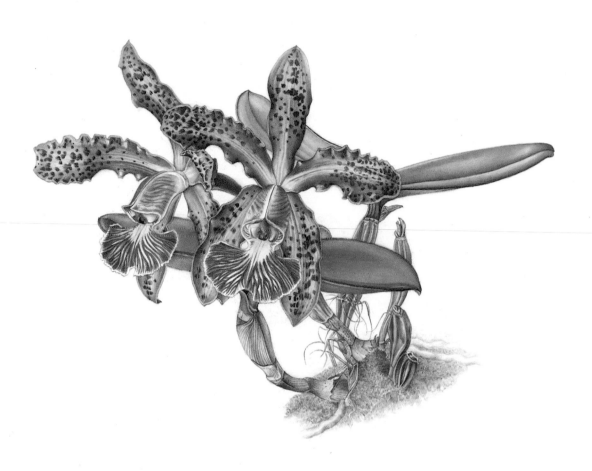

Cattleya schilleriana

Hiroe Sasaki
December 1994

Hippeastrum buds and seed capsule

Watercolour · 17 x 22.5cm

opposite

Paphiopedilum superbiens and *Calathea warscewiczii*

Watercolour · 24 x 14.5cm

SIRIOL SHERLOCK

Magnolia campbellii subsp. *mollicomata* 'Lanarth'

Watercolour · 66 x 53cm

This fabulous tree, originally a native of Yunnan and Burma grows to about 20m high. This particular variety grows in the Sir Harold Hillier Gardens and Arboretum, near Romsey in Hampshire. It was covered with hundreds of these huge unbelievably bright purplish-pink flowers in March/April this year. Magnolias with these distinctively shaped flowers are described as 'cup and saucer'. The large (10–25cm) leaves appear after the flowers are over.

Siriol Sherlock

SHEILA SIEGERMAN

Potinara di ciommo 'David'

Watercolour · 22.5 x 19cm

Patinata is a relatively new designation for a cross between four genera: *Cattelya, Brassavola, Sophronitis* and *Laelia*. This very beautiful new orchid was bred by a grower in Hamilton, Ontario. It has been named by the grower J. Di Ciommo for his son David.

Sheila Siegerman

NIKI SIMPSON

Ginkgo biloba L. · **Maidenhair Tree**

Watercolour and Pencil · 40 x 29cm

Summer twig showing both short spur shoots and long free-growing shoots x1, winter twig x1, woody spur shoot from female tree with developing fruit x1, detail of female flower x1, side and front view of nut x1, woody spur shoot from male tree with catkin-like male flowers x1, detail of male flower x2, detail of two views of stamen after dehiscence x5, detail of single leaf to show dichotomous venation x2.

Ginkgo (the Japanese name translates to 'Silver Apricot') was a widely distributed genus in prehistoric times but only a single species has survived to the present. *Ginkgo biloba* is a deciduous, dioecious tree growing up to 40 metres high. It is generally considered extinct in the wild but has been preserved and is still grown in temple gardens and as a specimen tree. It is unique among gymnosperms in having leaves with dichotomous venation. With its distinctive fan shaped leaves, its wonderful yellow autumn colour and its ability to tolerate environmental pollution, *Ginkgo biloba* has been increasingly planted in urban landscape schemes. Its fleshy fruits have a very unpleasant smell on ripening; each contains a large edible nut. The roasted kernels are considered a delicacy in Eastern Asia. The *Ginkgoa* has long been used in China for medicinal purposes and numerous active constituents have been extracted from the leaves.

CHRISTINE STEPHENSON

'Auriculas'

Watercolours · both 18.5 x 15cm

In 1939 Sacheverell Sitwell wrote, 'The first moment of seeing an auricula is an experience never to be forgotten. It would seem incredible that a flower, through human skill, should attain this degree of natural or trained artificiality. For the perfection of the auricula is that of the most exquisite Meissen porcelain, of the most lovely stuffs of Isfahan, which is to say that it attains to the highest technical standards of human craftsmanship. And yet, it is a living and growing thing with the gift of procreation.'

Auriculas have been cultivated for at least 400 years. Prized almost as jewels by the upper classes of

the seventeenth century, and from the eighteenth century treasured by the 'Florist's Societies' who cultivated the decorative flowering plants and grew them to a high standard of excellence. Enthusiasm for the show varieties reached its peak in the nineteenth century, particularly in the north of England.

The auriculas we see today are the result of many years of dedicated cultivation by a few enthusiasts, and the signs are that they are beginning to create a great deal of popular interest once again.

In my paintings of auriculas, I have tried to illustrate the 'ideal' characteristics of each type, and to suggest the rich and decorative colours of the flowers, against the varied leaf forms and farina textures of these quaint, and most delightful plants.

JUDI STONE

Cypripedium parviflorum var. pubescens · Yellow Lady's Slipper Orchid
Watercolour · 40 x 31cm

The large yellow lady's slipper is the most common lady's slipper species found in North America, where it is distributed across the continent. Easily recognised by its yellow pouch, it is characterised by its wavy sepals and long twisted petals, of a lime green colour finely veined with reddish brown. These particular plants form a spectacular large clump growing on pastureland in Northern Alberta, Canada, and were seen flowering in the month of July.

J.Stope

JESSICA TCHEREPNINE

Onions

Watercolour · 32.5 x 23cm

Onions are a member of plant genus *Allium* the same family as the chive, *A. schoenoprasum*, garlic, *A. sativum*, leek, *A. porrum*, and shallot, *A. ascalonium.*

The earliest evidence of onion cultivation began at the edges of the Mediterranean around 3,000 BC and the evidence has been found of onions left in Egyptian tombs since about *c*.2,500 BC. Paintings of onions appear on the inner walls of the pyramids of Unas, *c*.2423 BC and Pepi II, *c*.2200 BC and in tombs of both the Old and New Kingdom. Many early documents tell of onion cultivation and use. There is evidence that the Sumerians were growing onions as early as 2500 BC. Texts from India dated to the early 6th century write of the onion's use as a medicine. They were used as a diuretic, and taken for the heart, the eyes and the joints.

The word onion derives from the Latin word Unio, meaning large pearl.

Jessica Tcherepnine
1998

JONATHAN TYLER

Himalayan *Cimbidium* Orchid

Watercolour · 55 × 42cm

I first painted this *Cymbidium* Orchid, from the
temperate forests at mid-altitude in the Himalaya
Mountains, at college in the early 90's, and recently,
to my delight, it flowered profusely and I set to work
again. It was quite a challenge, taking 170 hours, the
linear leaves and creamy flowers demanding a great
deal of tiny brush-strokes to achieve the required
smoothness. It is never easy to do full justice to these
exotic orchids; however I was very satisfied with the
result.

J.P.Tyler

Himalayan Cymbidium Orchid. © Jonathan R Tyler 2003

WENDY WALSH

Crocosmia masoniorum 'Rowallane Yellow'

Watercolour · 45 x 28cm

The most familiar plant in the genus *Crocosmia* is the weedy, scarlet-orange blossomed montbretia, *Crocosmia* x *crocosmiiflora*, which is abundant in ditches and roadsides in western Ireland and Britain. That plant, a hybrid artificially produced in France in the 1870s, is a naturalised 'garden escape'.

Crocosmia comprises about ten species, all native in Africa. *Crocosmia masoniorum* is a fine, stately plant that is native in a small and relatively inaccessible area of the southern Drakensburg Mountains in South Africa. It is believed to be rare in the wild. Its name is a tribute to the Revd Edward Mason and his sister Marianne who collected the species in the Drakensburg Mountains in the early 1900s.

This cultivar arose by chance in the garden at Rowallane House, Saintfield, County Down, Northern Ireland, sometime in the late 1970s. It was illustrated and named in 1983 by the eminent English horticulturist Graham Stuart Thomas in his book *Gardens of the National Trust*. Rowallane is one of the National Trust's finest gardens, especially renowned for its rhododendrons.

Crocosmia masoniorum 'Rowallane Yellow' is a robust, perennial, deciduous herb with an underground corm. The leaves are sword-shaped, pleated, about 1m long, and arranged in a fan. The large amber-yellow flowers have six petals, and are arranged, in pairs, on the upper side of the curved stem.

Wendy Walsh 1999

CAROL WOODIN

Dendrobium cuthbertsonii

Watercolour on Vellum · 11 x 18.5cm

The plant originates in Papua, New Guinea, and
grows in cloud forests at 6000–9000 feet in elevation.
These areas are cool and humid with little seasonal
variation. The red-orange variety shown is the most
common variety, although they are found in colours
from a creamy-yellow to coral to bi-colours as well.
The gentleman who grows these lovely plants is
Darrin Norton. His greenhouse in Vermont is a
beautiful respite from the howling winds of winter.

FATIMA ZAGONEL

Tibouchina pulchra (Cham) Cogn. 'Quaresmeira'
Watercolour · 26 x 27.5cm

Medium to high tree occurring in the Atlantic rain-forests of Brazil. 5–15m in height with white bark. Broad or subreflexed leaves, 6–8cm length, 2–3cm width; concave bracts, deciduous, dorsally cinereous, 16–18mm length, 10–12mm width. Campanulate greyish calyx with a narrow base and widened ciliate apex; broad white petals becoming red-violet, 3.5–4cm length. Slightly flexuous stamens, purple, 10–12mm length; flexible purple anthers. Subglobose capsule with yellowish seeds. This sample was taken from the Sapitanduva preservation area, Antonina, Paran, Brazil.

Melastomaceae

Tibouchina pulchra (Cham.) Cogn.

M. Fatima Zagonel.

South Brazil, January 2000.

Artists' Biographies

Gillian Barlow

After studying art at the Slade and attaining a BA
and MA in History of Art at the University of Sussex,
Gillian Barlow pursued a career in fine art which
eventually led her to botanical painting. The first
public airing of her botanical work was at a Linnean
Society group exhibition in 1990 and she has exhibited extensively since. Her work has been included in
three of the Hunt Institute's exhibitions, in '92, '96
and 2000 and her work has been consistently shown
and honoured at the Royal Horticultural Society and
the Society of Botanical Artists. In 1995 she had a solo
exhibition at Spink's in London and her work was
represented the following year in the touring exhibition of the Shirley Sherwood Collection. She has
produced paintings for *Curtis's Botanical Magazine*
and *The New Plantsman* and her work as a Heraldic
Painter at the College of Arms in London, is repro
duced in *Heraldry*, London, 1993, and *The Art of
Heraldry*, London, 1998. She teaches botanical
painting at the English Gardening School, based at
the Chelsea Physic Garden, London. Public and
private collections of her work include, The British
Council, Vassar College, New York and the Shirley
Sherwood Collection.

Mary Bates

Mary Bates (also working as Mary Mendum) graduated in Zoology from the University of Leeds in 1967. She worked from 1967–71 as Scientific Assistant at the CSIRO Division of Entomology and School of Biological Science, Canberra, Australia. Her work as a freelance botanical artist began in 1979 though since 1987 she has worked either part or full time at the Royal Botanic Garden, Edinburgh.

Her work has been widely published particularly in relation to the genus *Aeschynanthus* (Gesneriaceae) and also in her contributions to journals such as *Curtis's Botanical Magazine* and *The New Plantsman*. Her exhibitions include Inverleith House, Edinburgh; Kew Gardens Gallery and the 6th International Exhibition of Botanical Art at the Hunt Institute, Pittsburgh, USA. In 1993 she received the Jill Smythies award for Botanical Illustration, given by the Linnean Society for her outstanding contribution to the art. She has tutored a number of courses in botanical illustration and continues to travel extensively in connection with her work as a scientific illustrator.

Mary Chambers Bauschelt

Mary Chambers Bauschelt was born in Milwaukee, Wisconsin, USA, 25th October, 1956. Growing up in a rural area, she was interested in woodland plants and flowers. After studying botany and horticulture, Mary received a BS in Horticulture in 1978 from the University of Wisconsin-Madison. Since 1981 she has been employed by the University of Wisconsin-Madison, Department of Botany Greenhouses and Botanical Garden. She is presently the Senior Horticulturist.

In 1994, after taking continuing education courses in biological illustration, she pursued and obtained a Certificate of Botanical Art and Illustration from the Morton Arboretum in Lisle, Illinois, in 1996. She is a member of the American Society of Botanical Artists and the Guild of Natural Science Illustrators. Most of her work is done in watercolour or pen-and-ink. She recently won an award at the Art In Science exhibition that was held in conjunction with the XVIth International Botanical Congress held at the Missouri Botanical Garden, St. Louis, Missouri, USA, in 1999.

Mary was included in the 9th International Exhibition of Botanical Art and Illustration held at the Hunt Institute for Botanical Documentation, Pittsburgh, USA in 1998.

Hendrieke Berg

Hendrieke Berg was born in 1964 in the Netherlands. After an education at a college studying arts and crafts she moved to Norway where she now lives. She has worked since 1987 as an artist from her studio in Norway since 1987 with a particular interest in glass engraving which she studied in San Diego. Her work in botanical illustration began in 1991 when she worked on drawings for the Flora of Peru at the Missouri Botanical Gardens, USA.

Following a course in Systematics at the Botanical Institute in Bergen, Norway in 1993 she worked at the Royal Botanic Gardens, Kew and studied at West Dean College. In the same year she began to prepare scientific drawings for Prof. Dr C. C. Berg botanist and scientist in tropical plants. In 1994 she made a trip to Ecuador to study tropical plants in their natural environments combined with illustration work on the collected material at the University of Quito, Ecuador. She has been engaged since in painting a collection of *Rhododendron* and other plants found naturally in Norway. She is currently working on an illustration for *Curtis's Botanical Magazine*.

Leslie Berge

Of French descent, Leslie Berge was born in Taunton, Massachusetts, USA in 1959. She began her formal art education at age eight and majored in the visual arts throughout secondary school. She holds a degree in Painting from Bennington College, graduating in 1981. She earned an Illustration degree from The Art Institute of Boston in 1983. Her education also includes a year abroad at The American College in Paris from 1979–80.

While a student in Paris, Leslie frequented the Jardin des Plantes, and subsequently took up botanical illustration in 1981. In 1984, under the auspices of The Thistle Gallery, Tiverton, RI, she was an instructor of painting and drawing. There she had a solo exhibition of her work, which was later published as a series of greeting cards. She works in watercolour and colour pencil, and for subject matter, tends towards the more tropical and exotic.

Her work has been exhibited world-wide, and can be found in numerous private collections throughout the USA, Europe and South Africa. Her illustrations are represented in the permanent collections of the Hunt Institute for Botanical Documentation, and The Shirley Sherwood Collection. Leslie is an active member in the American Society of Botanical Artists, the Guild of Natural Science Illustrators, and exhibits annually at Denver Botanic Gardens where she has received several awards. She began a study of *Cycads* in 1997, illustrating ten species of this primitive plant group, which included travels to South Africa in 1998. Her bibliography includes the Hunt Institute's 7th International Exhibition of Botanical Art & Illustration, 1992, and Contemporary Botanical Artists: The Shirley Sherwood Collection, 1996.

Jenny Brasier

Jenny Brasier received no formal training but has relied on two close friends for help and encouragement. The late Wilfred Blunt who was a constant influence and inspiration to her and John Whitehead, plant explorer, who also encouraged her with constructive criticism, endless patience and a supply of rare plants from around the world.

She has specialised in the illustration of the genus Hosta and the different forms of species cyclamen. Her work has been widely exhibited at among others, The Smithsonian Institution in Washington, The Natural History Museum in London, The Hunt Institute for Botanical Documentation in Pittsburgh, The Royal Botanic Gardens at Kew and The Victoria and Albert Museum, London. She has received numerous honours for her work, particularly for her pencil drawings and work on vellum.

Andrew Brown

Andrew Brown Graduated in 1969 from St Catherine's College, Oxford with a BA Hons in Botany and later gained a PhD from Clare Hall Cambridge. He has been exhibiting his botanical work since 1980, regularly at the Carleton Gallery of Westminster School where he teaches and also with the Royal Horticultural Society from whom he has received two gold medals. He has also had solo exhibitions at the Linnean Society in London and Wolfson College, Oxford. He has been included in two exhibitions at the Hunt Institute for Botanical Documentation in Pittsburgh and two exhibitions at Kew Gardens Gallery including the exhibition of the Shirley Sherwood Collection.

His published work includes, *The Flora of Oxfordshire* (six plates), Pisces Press, 1998; *Wildlife guide to ferns*, BBC *Wildlife Magazine*, September 1998, *Curtis's Botanical Magazine* and *Garden of World Medicine*, Chelsea Physic Garden, 1998. He is First Fellow of the Chelsea Physic Garden Florilegium Society which is producing a modern florilegium for the garden and eight of his illustrations are held in the archive of the Physic Garden. His illustrations are also held in the collections of the Hunt Institute, The Shirley Sherwood Collection, Westminster School and many private collections.

Pauline Dean

Pauline Dean was born in Brighton and studied 'A' level Art and Botany at school, prior to training as a nurse. When nursing ended after marriage in 1968 four children were added to the home over the course of the next ten years, and she was kept fully occupied. In 1984 she commenced serious painting and now specialises in botanically accurate Watercolour paintings and also works in Pen and Ink.

She tutors Botanical Art at Wisley Gardens and is the holder of six Gold Medals from the Royal Horticultural Society. The latest being for a series of waterlilies shown in December 1999. During the year, her work was also part of two further multiple exhibits that received Gold Medals. In 1998 she featured in *The Tortworth Chestnut* – one of the BBC 2 series, *Meetings with Remarkable Trees*. In 1997 Pauline had a solo exhibition at Guildford House Gallery and for the whole of 1996 her work was displayed in the Director General's Office of the RHS.

She designed the three winter plates in the RHS's *Collectors' Series* and the 1996 Chelsea Flower Show plate. In addition to undertaking private commissions, Pauline's illustrations are regularly published in scientific journals and horticultural books.

Her paintings are in collections world-wide including the Shirley Sherwood Collection of Contemporary Botanical Artists, the Museum of Wales, the Linnean Society, the RHS Lindley Library, the Royal Botanic Gardens, Kew, the Chelsea Physic Garden and the Hunt Institute of Botanical Documentation, Pittsburgh, USA.

Elvia Esparza

Since 1981 Elvia Esparza has been Scientific Illustrator at the Institute of Biology and teacher of Biological Illustration at the Faculty of Sciences at UNAM, Mexico City. She is well known for her work in the many volumes of *The Flora of Veracruz*. She is the founder and President of the Mexican Academy of Scientific Illustration. Her work is well known and widely exhibited in her native Mexico and has recently been exhibited at the 9th Annual Exhibition of the Hunt Institute for Botanical Documentation, Pittsburgh, USA and in an exhibition at the Natural History Museum in London entitled *Images of Mexican biodiversity*.

Annie Farrer

In 1974 Ann Farrer commenced work for the Royal
Botanic Garden, Kew, working on numerous floras
including; *Flora Zambesiaca, Flora of Tropical East
Africa, Flora of Aldabra* and also the Kew Bulletin.
In 1977 she received a Churchill Travelling Fellowship to go over-land to the Himalayas to draw for a
book *Flowers of the Himalayas*. Other books she has
worked on include, *Flora of the Balkans, Vegetation
of Europe, Docks and Knotweeds* (Botanical Society
of the British Isles), *Umbellifers* (B S B I), *Collins
Field Guide to the Grasses, Sedges, Rushes and Ferns
of Britain and Northern Europe* and the Kew Monograph on *Arum*, among others.

Her work has appeared in *Flower Artists of Kew*
and *The Shirley Sherwood Collection of Contemporary Botanical Artists*. In 1991 she produced a series of
six paintings from the endangered rainforests which
were published by Kew as prints. She has been a
regular contributor to *Curtis's Botanical Magazine*
and was the first recipient of the Jill Smythies award
for botanical illustration from the Linnean Society.
She has received six Gold Medals from the RHS and
painted orchids for the orchid committee.

She has exhibited extensively including at the Kew
Gardens Gallery. Her work is held in the collections
of the RHS Lindley Library, The Hunt Institute,
Pittsburgh, The Shirley Sherwood Collection and
many other private and public collections world-wide.

She teaches the Kew two-week course on botanical
illustration and at the Chelsea Physic Gardens London. She was also trek leader for *Exodus Expeditions*
between 1984–97, mainly to the Himalayas. She has
recently completed 148 pages of drawings for the
Grasses of Bolivia, (RBG Kew) and is presently working on a monograph of *Biarum* for Kew and a series
of thirty *Arisaemas* for a private collector.

Georita Harriott

Georita Harriott graduated in 1994 from Middlesex
University with a BA Hons in scientific illustration
and in 1995 from Cambridge University with a PGCE
in art. Following her graduation she received a
commission from the Royal Zoological Society to
paint insects for the new Insect House at Regent's
Park Zoo. She devised and taught a Natural History
Drawing course for Madingley Hall, Cambridge
University, and she continues to teach this course. In
1995 she had a solo exhibition of insect and flower
paintings at the Linnean Society, London. She has
worked as an illustrator for, among others, The
Botanical Gardens, Cambridge; The Zoology
Museum, Cambridge; The Royal Horticultural
Society and for *Curtis's Botanical Magazine*. Her
work is represented in the collections of The Hunt
Institute for Botanical Documentation, Pittsburgh,
USA.

Christina Hart-Davies

Christina Hart-Davies was born and brought up in the English Midlands. After reading Fine Art and Typography at Reading University she worked for several years with a London design group, being mainly responsible for the design and production of educational books. In 1975, after a time spent sailing and travelling in Europe and North Africa, she settled in Dorset and began to combine her twin interests of painting and natural history. She paints plant portraits, life size on the paper and habitats in miniature on vellum.

She has held many exhibitions in Britain and abroad and her work is included in many collections world-wide, notably the Hunt Institute and the collection of Shirley Sherwood. She has illustrated many books including, *A Year in the Victorian Garden* and *The Green Guide to Herbs*. She has contributed illustrations to *Curtis's Botanical Magazine*, *The Royal Horticultural Society's New Dictionary of Gardening*, the BBC *Wildlife Magazine* and many others. She frequently illustrates rare plants for Plantlife, the wild plant conservation charity.

She has a special interest in mosses and lichens and her work on these subjects has several times been awarded the Gold Medal of the Royal Horticultural Society. She also holds an RHS Gold Medal and a World Orchid Conference Bronze for her paintings of Australian and European native orchids.

She is a committed member of several conservation organisations and has travelled extensively in Europe, Australia and the Americas to study and paint the native flora. In 1993 she joined an expedition to Sumatra to paint plants of the rainforest and mountain areas and some of the resulting paintings were included in a three artist exhibition at Kew in 1994.

Whenever possible Christina paints from life and she has worked in a great variety habitats. Subject matter is drawn from the cultivated or exotic specimens as well as from native flora.

Jenny Jowett

Jenny Jowett has painted seriously since childhood, specialising in botanical work for the last fifteen years. When only twelve she won a national painting competition and on leaving school was accepted by the Slade College of Art. However, her keen interest in agriculture and botany persuaded her to take an NDD at Studley College, Warwickshire.

In 1974 she started painting professionally, working from her home in Hampshire where her garden provided her with inspiration and much of her painting material.

She is a founder member of the Society of Botanical Artists, and has won three gold medals, three silver gilt medals and two silver medals from the Royal Horticultural Society. She also designed the RHS Chelsea plate for 1992. Her paintings have been reproduced in the recently published books *The White Garden* and *The Glory of the English Garden*. She is currently illustrating a book for the Royal Botanic Gardens, Kew on the genus *Paeonia* and works for *Curtis's Botanical Magazine* and *The Plantsman*. She studied lithography and from 1978–82 published hand drawn lithographs for Christies Contemporary Art, London on her own litho proofing press.

In 1986 she was invited to take over the botanical illustration course run annually by the British Field Studies Council at Flatford Mill, thereby becoming only the third person to occupy this unique position since John Nash who created the course in 1947. She runs water colour workshops during the year from her studio at home and lectures widely in her particular interest of botanical illustration and plants.

Her work is hanging in several public collections, including the Lindley Library, London, the Hunt Institute for Botanical Documentation, Pittsburgh, USA and in private collections throughout the UK, China, Japan, USA and South Africa. She has had many joint exhibitions and ten solo exhibitions.

Christabel King

Christabel King graduated in Botany from the University of London and studied Scientific Illustration at Middlesex University. She made her first painting for *Curtis's Botanical Magazine* in 1975 and has continued to produce illustrations for this and other publications of the Royal Botanic Gardens, Kew. Her work includes monographs of various plant genera such as *Pleione*, *Lewisia*, *Echinisereus*, *Cleistocactus* (unpublished) and *Galanthus*, which is shortly to be published by Timber Press.

In 1987 she took part in an exhibition to the Ruwenzori Mountains of Uganda to paint the afro-alpine flora for the book *Africa's Mountains of the Moon* by Guy Yeoman, Elm Tree Books 1990. Her paintings were included in the exhibition *Three Continents* at the Kew Gardens Gallery in 1993. She was awarded the Jill Smythies Prize for Botanical Illustration in 1989 by the Linnean Society of London. Since 1990 she has been acting as tutor for the botanical artists of Brazil studying at Kew under the scholarship scheme set up in memory of Margaret Mee. In 1994 she visited Brazil and gave courses in botanical illustration in Rio de Janeiro, São Paulo and at Caxiuana in Paraguay where she was also able to make paintings herself of the flowers of the rain forest. During term time she teaches at Capel Manor College, Enfield, Middlesex.

Her work is represented in the library of the Royal Botanic Gardens, Kew; the Hunt Institute; the Shirley Sherwood Collection and other private collections.

Deborah Lambkin

Deborah Lambkin was born in Cork, and raised in Dublin, Ireland. She has been drawing and painting since her childhood and has always had a keen interest in gardens and nature. For her degree in Visual Communication at the National College of Art and Design, Dublin, in 1990, she wrote a thesis on botanical art. Inspired and encouraged by Wendy Walsh, the octogenarian doyen of botanical painting in Ireland, Deborah has been painting botanical works ever since.

She has undertaken many commissions, most notably for the National Botanic Gardens, Dublin, Dublin City University, Kew Magazine and The National Trust Northern Ireland. She has painted a series of paintings of endangered Irish wildflowers used as posters for schools. In 1997–8 she spent eighteen months working on a series of 21 paintings of *Vireya* Rhododendrons growing at the National Botanic Gardens. All but one are in the Gardens collection. The remaining painting is in the Royal Botanic Garden, Edinburgh.

Deborah has exhibited in London several times, with the Society of Botanical Artists and at the Royal Horticultural Society, where she has received two silver (1997–8) and one gold medal (1999). She has had two solo exhibitions, one at the National Botanic Gardens, Dublin and one at the Royal Hibernian Hotel, Dublin. Most recently Deborah has been accepted as a member of the prestigious Watercolour Society of Ireland and her work resides in the permanent collection in Co. Limerick. She also exhibits at their annual exhibitions.

Joanna Asquith Langhorne

Joanna Langhorne was born in Buckinghamshire in 1945 and moved with her parents to Lancashire three years later. She was especially fascinated by art and biology at school and was encouraged in these interests by her father, the painter and designer, John Asquith Langhorne. With him she attended several Field Studies Courses at Flatford Mill, East Bergholt. Her tutor was the renowned painter John Nash CBE, RA 1893–1977. She attended the Central School of Arts and Crafts, London between 1963 and 1965. After college she began working for the Freshwater Biological Association, Bowness-on-Windermere. Here she worked under Dr T.T. Macan, the distinguished entomologist. She drew and illustrated fishes, insects and freshwater invertebrates. In 1973 she was appointed the *official artist-in residence* at the Royal Botanic Gardens, Kew. She left Kew after seven years in order to move to Windermere to take on freelance commissions. Among these were twelve designs for plates to commemorate the 250th anniversary of Kew for Royal Doulton. She later moved to a remote village near the Lake District village of Wasdale. Here she grew a variety of unusual plants for painting and purely for botanical interest – especially alpines and woodland plants. She is now living and working near Kew in Richmond where she continues to work on illustration for scientific journals and publications as well as individual commissions and paintings for exhibitions.

She has completed a large body of illustrative work including complete illustrations for *Vegetation of East Africa*, E.M. Lind, Longmans, 1974; *Gardeners' Book of Trees*, A. Mitchell, Dent, 1981; *In Search of the Wild Asparagus* – Roy Lancaster, Rainbird, 1983; *Conifers*, K. Rushforth, Croom Helm 1987 and *The Hardy Euphorbias*, R. Turner, Batsford, 1995. She has also contributed illustration to numerous publications notably; *Orchid's from Curtis's Botanical Magazine*, Curwen Press 1979; *The Crocus*, Brian Mathew, Batsford 1982; *The Genus Paphiopedilum*, P. Cribb, Kew 1988; *The Flower Artists of Kew*, Herbert Press, 1992 and *Contemporary Botanical Artists, The Shirley Sherwood Collection*, Wiedenfeld & Nicholson, 1996. Her work has always featured prominently in *The New Plantsman, Curtis's Botanical Magazine* and *The Kew Bulletin*.

She has exhibited widely since 1980 and these exhibitions include, The Brewery Art Centre, Kendal Museum of Natural History 1981; Lowe's Court Gallery, Egremont, Cumbria 1983; The Royal Horticultural Society (Lindley Medal) 1986; The Chelsea Physic Garden 1988; The Hunt Institute for Botanical Documentation, Pittsburgh 1974; The British Museum, *Flowers in Art from East and West*, 1975; The Royal Botanic Garden, Edinburgh/Scottish Arts Council; The Royal Botanic Gardens, Kew – with Christabel King and Jessica Tcherepnine 1993. She was represented in the exhibition of the Shirley Sherwood Collection of Botanical Art at the Kew Gardens Gallery, 1996.

Her work is held in many private and public collections world wide.

Polly Morris

Polly Morris completed the Certificate in Botanical Illustration from the University of Sheffield in 1996. In February 1997 she was awarded a Royal Horticultural Society Silver Medal for her display of botanical paintings, *A Year in the Garden*. She has exhibited at Harlow Carr Fuchsia Festival in 1998 and the Natural History Museum in London in 1999. She is a keen gardener, and provides illustrations for the journal of the Mediterranean Garden Society.

She has studied Calligraphy and Lettering at the Roehampton Institute, London, and has completed the Advanced Training Scheme of the Society of Scribes and Illuminators. In 1992 she won first prize in the National Osmiroid *Spirit of the Letter* competition. She has exhibited work at the SSI *Celebration of Calligraphy* 75th Anniversary Exhibition at Leighton House, London, Bolton Art Gallery in 1996, the SSI *Calligraphy 97* Exhibition at Durham Light Infantry Museum and Leamington Art Gallery in 1997 and at the *Belle Lettere* International Exhibition in Padua, Italy, in 1997.

Luca Palermo

Luca Palermo was born in Rome in 1956 and following the family profession, graduated in medicine from the University of Rome. His interest in natural sciences stems from his childhood. A visit to the exhibition, *Flowers in Art from the East and West*, at the British Museum in 1984 galvanised his resolve to concentrate on the painting of plants and to study the history of botanical painting.

His interest in the historical aspect of his work extends to his use of the most traditional materials. He prepares many of his own pigments with great concern for their durability and purity. He also is closely involved with the nurture of the specimens he paints.

He has exhibited extensively world-wide and his work is represented in the Royal Collection at Windsor, the Fitzwilliam Museum, Cambridge and the Shirley Sherwood Collection.

He is the instructor of botanical drawing at the University of Rome.

Kathy Pickles

Kathy Pickles was born in London and has lived in Orkney for the past eighteen years, where she has had a number of solo exhibitions since 1988. She has exhibited five times at the Royal Horticultural Society's Westminster Flower Shows since 1991, on each occasion being awarded the Society's Gold Medal for botanical painting. As a result of this, she was invited to produce a painting for the 1997 Chelsea Flower Show Plate, which celebrated the Golden Wedding Anniversary of the Queen and Prince Philip.

In November 1995 she took part in a three-person show at the Royal Botanic Gardens' Gallery at Kew. She has also exhibited in mixed shows in Edinburgh, the Scottish Borders and the Hunt Institute in Pittsburgh. Examples of her work have been purchased for the Royal Botanic Gardens of Kew and Edinburgh, the RHS Lindley Library, the Hunt Institute for Botanical Documentation and the Shirley Sherwood Collection.

Bryan Poole

Bryan Poole is a New Zealand born Natural History and Botanical artist who has been working in Great Britain since the early 1980's. He has worked for among others: *The British Homeopathic Journal*, The World Wide Fund for Nature, The Natural History Museum, London and MacMillan Press Publications for the Royal Horticultural Society. He is also a regular contributor to the *Weekend Financial Times* and the *Independent on Sunday*.

His formal training as a botanical artist stems from his association with the Royal Botanic Gardens, Kew where he worked under Dr Christopher Grey-Wilson, former editor of the *Kew Magazine* and numerous other works on botanical and horticultural subjects.

His work now is almost exclusively devoted to the process of etching in the traditional manner.

Valerie Price

Valerie Price has worked as a freelance botanical illustrator since graduating from a degree course at Middlesex University specialising in Scientific Illustration. Her work is well known to readers of *Curtis's Botanical Magazine*, *The Plantsman* and many other related publications. Her place in William Stearn's *Flower Artists of Kew* places her firmly in the forefront of contemporary botanical illustration. Her work was included in the 9th Annual exhibition at the Hunt Institute, Pittsburgh, USA.

Rodella Purves

Rodella Purves was born in Paisley, Renfrewshire in 1945. She was educated in Edinburgh and graduated with a diploma in agricultural botany, followed by a diploma in seed testing at the National Institute of Agriculture in Cambridge. She worked until 1968 for the Department of Agriculture in Scotland as a seed analyst and then spent a year in New Zealand also as a seed analyst. She returned to Edinburgh and from 1969–76 worked for the Royal Botanic Garden as an exhibition designer and illustrator. Since then, and as the pressures of a family have allowed, she has worked as a botanical painter and illustrator.

Her work is known to a wide audience and she began exhibiting in 1975 with work included in a Scottish Arts Council exhibition, *From Sowerby, Bauer, Hooker and Fitch; Botanical Illustrations from 1800 to the Present Day*. Her work was included in the *4th International Exhibition of Botanical Art* at the Hunt Institute, Pittsburgh, USA and a year later at the *International Exhibition of Botanical Drawings*, The Hunterdon Art Center, Clinton, New Jersey, USA. 1980 saw her work in *The Plant in 20th Century Botanical Illustration*, again for the Scottish Arts Council and in 1986 at the *Blumenlese: International Exhibition of Botanical Art*. Galerie Bartsch and Chariau, Munich, Germany. She has had a number of solo exhibitions at the Broughton Gallery, Biggar and in 1996 the City Art Centre, Edinburgh staged a major retrospective of her work, 'Rodella Purves, Botanical Paintings 1976–1996'.

Her work has been widely published notably in *Curtis's Botanical Magazine*; *The New Kew Magazine*; *The Plantsman*; *The New Plantsman* (Royal Horticultural Society) and *Country Life*. Books featuring her work include; *The Rhododendron Species*, H.H. Davidian, vols 1–4; *Flower Artists of Kew*, Herbert Press 1990; *The Orchid Book*, James Cullen, Cambridge University Press 1992; *The New R.H.S. Dictionary of Plants*, MacMillan, 1992 and *The European Garden Flora*, vol.5, 1997.

She was recently awarded the Jill Smythies Prize for Botanical Art by the Linnean Society.

Reinhild Raistrick

Reinhild Raistrick's great love is the illustration of wild flowers in the British Isles and abroad, particularly working in situ. She has spent much time in remoter parts of the world working in this way. For example, working in Tanzania on various species of the Saint paulia. A number of her paintings were purchased for the permanent collection at the Royal Botanic Gardens, Kew. Her work features in *Curtis's Botanical Magazine*, as well as other publications.

She is a regular exhibitor at the Royal Horticultural Society and has been awarded four Gold Medals; in 1992 for the series *Flowers of the African Rain Forest*; in 1994 for the series on *Wild Orchids of East Anglia*; and in 1996 for the series on *Fritillaria* from the Cambridge University Botanic Garden Collection; in 2000 for the series on *Galanthus* species and cultivars. In 1998, she was awarded a Silver Gilt Medal for her series on *Wild Flowers in Crete*. She is a member of the Society of Botanical Artists and exhibits annually at the Westminster Galleries, London.

Kay Rees-Davies

Kay Rees-Davies is a founder member and vice-president of the North Wales Society of Botanical and Fine Watercolour Artists and in 1996, 1998 and 1999 received the Society's award for Botanical Art. She is a member of the Botanical Artists of Ness Gardens and has recently been elected to serve on the Executive Committee. Her work has been shown at many group exhibitions including the Society of Botanical Artists, London; the Royal Birmingham Society of Artists; the Portico Library and Gallery, Manchester and at several Welsh galleries including Oriel Ynys Mon and Penrhyn Castle. She has exhibited several times at the Royal Horticultural Society. Her first solo exhibition was held at Bodnant Garden in March 1993 and subsequently at Penrhyn Castle in 1997, 1998 and 1999.

Two of her paintings are now in the permanent collection of the Hunt Institute. In 1996 the RHS purchased two of her paintings for the Lindley Library. These were part of an exhibition of *Ivies* from the national Hedera Collection shown at the RHS, for which she was awarded a Gold Medal. One of these was purchased for the Shirley Sherwood Collection. A second Gold Medal was awarded in 1998 for a series of paintings of *Old Apple Varieties*. She is a member of the Society of Botanical Artists and was awarded its Certificate of Botanical Merit in 1994.

Her work has been published in *An Introduction to Drawing Flowers* by Margaret Stevens; *Plantas Endemicas e Avores Indiginas de Carbo Verde* by T. Levens, 1995 Bonn University, Germany; *Contemporary Botanical Artists, The Shirley Sherwood Collection*, London 1996 and in *Curtis's Botanical Magazine* 1997.

She has been a tutor there for several years. She holds her own classes at Rhos-on-Sea, North Wales and has held workshops and day classes throughout the country.

Hiroe Sasaki

Born in Hiroshima, Japan, Hiroe Sasaki graduated from Nara University of Education where she specialised in Art. She has been living in Brazil since 1970. In 1991, as a Margaret Mee Botanical Foundation scholar, she studied Botanical Art under Christabel King's guidance. In 1995 she won first place in a competition for the poster for the 46th Botanical Congress. She works as a freelance artist, illustrating various school books and has also undertaken commissions for the University of São Paulo. She has taken part in various exhibitions.

Pandora Sellars

Pandora Sellars was born in Herefordshire in 1936. After a rural childhood and schooling she received her artistic education at Hereford and Cheltenham Schools of Art. She specialised in printed textiles but found herself drawn more towards the natural world of plants. Her husband shared her interests and she began to record in watercolour his collection of orchids. She exhibited these at the Royal Horticultural Society and was subsequently introduced to *Curtis's Botanical Magazine*, to which she is still a regular contributor.

She had a solo exhibition at the Kew Gallery in 1990 and has taken part in numerous other exhibitions in Britain and abroad. She illustrated the *Flora of Jersey* in 1984 and two Kew monographs, *The Genus Paphiopedilium* in 1987 and *The Genus Arum* in 1993. Her work is included in *The Flower Artists of Kew*, 1990 and *Contemporary Botanical Artists – The Shirley Sherwood Collection*, 1996.

She painted a design for a plate and a presentation picture for HRH The Princess of Wales to mark the opening of the new conservatory at Kew in 1987. In 1993 she designed a set of five postage stamps for the British Post Office. Her work is represented in numerous private and public collections.

Siriol Sherlock

Siriol Sherlock grew up in Hampshire and studied textile design at Winchester School of Art, obtaining her degree in 1977. After graduation she worked in the textile industry and as a freelance designer producing many floral furnishing designs for the world market.

In 1986 she began to exhibit her watercolour flower paintings and has exhibited continuously since then. She was elected to membership of The Society of Botanical Artists in 1988 and regularly shows at their Westminster Gallery exhibitions. Her work has been shown in The Royal Institute of Painters in Watercolour (RI) Exhibition and in solo shows at The Sir Harold Hillier Gardens Arboretum and The Kew Gardens Gallery. She is President of The Society of Floral Painters.

Siriol has been awarded three Royal Horticultural Society Gold Medals and two Silver Gilts and is a member of the Picture Committee which judges botanical art at the RHS shows. She has been commissioned to paint rare plants for *Curtis's Botanical Magazine* and *The New Plantsman* as well as for several eminent botanists. Her book *Exploring Flowers in Watercolour – Techniques and Images*, published by Batsford was voted 'Best Art Instruction Book of the Year' in 1988.

Although she is well known for her botanical work, Siriol considers herself to be 'a watercolour artist who paints flowers'. She rarely uses a pencil and likes to paint with fairly large brushes loaded with wet washes to capture the freshness and translucency of the flowers.

Sheila Siegerman

Sheila Siegerman's artistic career has been a varied one. Beginning in 1951 as a jewellery designer, switching to graphic design and back to jewellery design before becoming a theatrical designer in 1963. Her work as a botanical artist began in 1987. Since then she has exhibited with various galleries in her native Canada and regularly since 1992 with The Royal Horticultural Society in London where she has been honoured with Gold and Silver Gilt medals. Her work was represented at the 7th International Exhibition of Botanical Art at the Hunt Institute, Pittsburgh, USA in 1992 and also in a travelling exhibition of the Hunt's *Orchid Paintings* in 1993. She was among the artists included in the exhibition of the Shirley Sherwood Collection in 1995. Her most recent exhibition has been in January of this year for the *Artistry of Orchids* at the Smithsonian Institution in Washington.

Niki Simpson

The daughter of two architect parents who are keen gardeners, Niki Simpson has been fascinated by plants and has drawn them since childhood. She studied botany at university as part of her degree in environmental science. She then worked as an assistant Landscape Architect in Edinburgh, before moving abroad and bringing up a family. During the eighteen months spent in the USA and six years in Norway, she travelled extensively. Back in SE England, she worked freelance in environmental illustration and computer graphics for three years.

She joined the Botany Department of the Royal Horticultural Society at Wisley in 1993, to set up the Society's horticultural database. In September 1999 she left Wisley to work full-time as a freelance botanical artist.

She has had both watercolour paintings and ink drawings published in *The New Plantsman* (Royal Horticultural Society) and in *Curtis's Botanical Magazine*. She has exhibited at the 6th International Rock Garden Plant Show (AGS) held at Warwick University in 1991, at numerous RHS shows in London, at West Dean and at RHS Rosemoor in Devon. She is the holder of gold medals from both the RHS (1998) and the AGS (1991).

Her main interest lies in 'investigative' botanical illustration, especially dissection work, with all parts drawn to scale, although she is also interested in the design possibilities of botanical work. Her main plant interests are ferns, climbers, British natives, botanical oddities such as parasitic plants and plants of the family Lardizabalaceae.

Current work includes further watercolour commissions for *The New Plantsman*, a watercolour of *Epimedium mikinorii* (commissioned by the Japanese botanist after whom it is named), illustrations for two monographs to be published by the ICUC, illustrations for volume 6 of the *European Garden Flora* and a cover illustration of *Zizania latifolia* for the BSBI, together with various private commissions.

She has been teaching courses in Botanical Art for the RHS, both at Wisley and at Rosemoor in Devon, since 1998.

Christine Stephenson

Christine Stephenson was born in Winchester in 1937 and after gaining a diploma at Bournemouth College of Art she pursued a career in teaching. On retirement in 1993 she started to work with botanical subjects mainly on commission.

She has exhibited at the Royal Horticultural Society in London, gaining a Silver Medal in 1995 and Gold in 1996 and with the Society of Botanical Artists, from whom she received a certificate of merit in 1999. Her work has been exhibited in Suffolk where she now lives.

Judi Stone

Judi Stone is a freelance botanical illustrator living in Bromley. She was originally trained as a biochemist, being awarded a BSc in 1967, a PhD in 1970, and subsequently did research on novel methods of insect control. She still maintains her interest in science through working part-time for the Open University. She took up botanical illustration when her children were growing up and established herself in this area by gaining honours at the Royal Horticultural Society. Including a Gold Medal in 1999.

She now works regularly at the Royal Botanic Gardens, Kew doing both line drawings and paintings for their publications, including *Curtis's Botanical Magazine*, *The Kew Bulletin*, and numerous works on orchids from all over the world.

She recently had work selected for the 9th International Exhibition of Botanical Art and Illustration at the Hunt Institute for Botanical Documentation, Pittsburgh, USA. She also exhibits regularly at the Society of Botanical Artists, and examples of her work are held in private collections in Europe, America and Africa. She belongs to the Florilegium Society of the Chelsea Physic Garden, and teaches botanical illustration at Bromley Adult Education College.

Jessica Tcherepnine

Jessica Tcherepnine began exhibiting botanical paintings in 1982 with an exhibition at the Clarges Gallery in London. Her work was included in the Fifth International Exhibition of Botanical Art at the Hunt Institute, Pittsburgh in 1983 and in the same year she also had an exhibition at the Shepherd Gallery, New York where she has continued to exhibit. Subsequent exhibitions included The Horticultural Society of New York in 1984, the Hobhouse Gallery, London in 1986, Galerie Jean Francois et Phillipe Heim, Paris in 1992 and Christopher Wood Contemporary Art London, in 1994. Her most recent exhibition was at the Newhouse Galleries Inc, New York, 1999. As well as these solo exhibitions she has also participated in many group exhibitions, notably those of the American Society of Botanical Artists, of which she is a director and the exhibition of the Collection of Shirley Sherwood at the Kew Gardens Gallery in 1996. Awards for her work include a Gold Medal from the Royal Horticultural Society for a series of watercolours of wild flowers from New York State in 1998, first place at the Greater New York Orchid Show, 1988 and a Gold Medal from the Royal Horticultural Society for a series of watercolours or orchids in 1990. Her work is in the collections of The Hunt Institute for Botanical Documentation, Pittsburgh, USA, The British Museum (Natural History), London, The Royal Horticultural Society, Lindley Library, London and numerous Private Collections in America, Europe and the Middle East.

Jonathan Tyler

After fifteen years working as a chef Jonathan Tyler decided to pursue his joint passions in art and natural history. In 1992 he was accepted onto and completed the HND course in technical illustration (Natural History) at Bournemouth and Poole College of Art and Design, gaining four distinctions.

In 1995, now working freelance, he completed his first commission (a fungi poster) for the BBC *Wildlife Magazine*. He was accepted onto an MA course in natural history illustration at the Royal College of Art, London and during this time he was awarded a Silver Gilt Medal for the work he exhibited at the RHS exhibition; eight orchid paintings completed during the HND.

Jonathan retired from the course in 1996 and started work on a series of thirteen orchid paintings for the Orchid Festival at the Royal Botanic Gardens, Kew. He exhibited at Kew from Feb–July 1997 and continued to work on a growing number of private commissions. In 1998 he completed a second poster (orchids) for the BBC *Wildlife Magazine*.

As well as working on pictures for the gallery, Jonathan is currently engaged on a long term project, namely the illustration of the entire montane flora of the British Isles. He has received a commission to work for *Curtis's Botanical Magazine*.

Wendy Walsh

Wendy Walsh was born in Cumbria, England on 9th April 1915 but for the last forty years has lived and worked in Ireland. She has exhibited extensively in England, Ireland and internationally, and has received many honours and awards. She is widely known for her stamp designs, and illustration of botanical books, with texts by Dr E. Charles Nelson, formerly taxonomist at the National Botanic Gardens, Glasnevin. In 1997 she was given an Honorary DLitt by the University of Dublin and in 1998 made a Life Member of the Royal Dublin Society.

She has received many awards throughout her career including; Royal Horticultural Society – Grenfell Silver Gilt Medal in 1977; Royal Horticultural Society Gold Medal in 1980, 1988 and 1994; Alpine Garden Society – Gold Award in 1991 and 1993 and Royal Horticultural Society of Ireland – Medal of Honour 1996.

Her exhibitions include; Melbourne, Australia; Dublin, Royal Hibernian Academy & Oireachtas; London, Royal Horticultural Society; Botanical Society of the British Isles; Hunt Institute for Botanical Documentation, Pittsburgh, USA; Watercolour Society of Ireland 1979–99 and The Royal Botanic Gardens, Kew, 1992.

Her work is widely published and includes: *An Irish Florilegium, Wild and Garden Flowers of Ireland*, London, Thames and Hudson. Vol.1. Wendy Walsh, Ruth Isabel Ross and E. Charles Nelson 1983. Vol.2. Wendy Walsh and E. Charles Nelson 1988; E. Charles Nelson *An Irish Flower Garden*, Kilkenny, Boethius Press, 1984; E. Charles Nelson and Eileen M. McCracken, *The Brightest Jewel – a History of the National Botanic Gardens, Dublin*, Kilkenny, Boethius Press 1987, four watercolours; Elizabeth Healey, Christopher Moriarty and Gerard O'Flaherty, *The Book of the Liffey from Source to Sea*, Dublin, Wolfhound Press, 1988. Chinese Ink drawings of six wild flowers; Wendy F. Walsh and E. Charles Nelson. *A Prospect of Irish Flowers*, Belfast, Blackstaff Press,

fine limited edition (125) 1990; E. Charles Nelson and Wendy F. Walsh, *The Burren, A Companion to the Wild Flowers of Ireland's Limestone Wilderness*, Kilkenny, Boethius Press 1991; E. Charles Nelson and Wendy F. Walsh, *Trees of Ireland, Native and Naturalized*, Dublin, Lilliput Press 1993; Edited by E. Charles Nelson, *16 watercolours by Wendy F. Walsh Flowers of Mayo*; *Dr. Patrick Browne's Fasciculus Plantaium Hiberniae 1788*. Fine limited edition (125), Dublin, Edmund Burke Publisher 1995; E. Charles Nelson & Wendy F. Walsh, *An Irish Flower Garden Replanted*, Dublin, Edmund Burke Publisher 1997; Illustrations in *The Kew Magazine, Curtis's Botanical Magazine, The Plantsman* and *The New Plantsman*. William T. Stearn, *Flower Artists of Kew, Botanical paintings by Contemporary Artists*, London, The Herbert Press in collaboration with The Royal Botanic Gardens, Kew 1990; James White & Donald E. Lendel, *Sixth International Exhibition of Botanical Art & Illustration*, Pittsburgh Hunt Institute for Botanical Documentation, Carnegie Mellon University 1998.

Carol Woodin

Carol Woodin was born in Salamanca, New York in 1956. Her career as a botanical artist began in 1992 when she began to show her work with orchids at the Eastern Orchid Congress, Boston, USA. Since then she has exhibited widely and notable exhibitions include: The World Orchid Congress in Glasgow Scotland in 1993, The Greater New York Orchid Society from 92–98; The Horticultural Society of New York and the Royal Horticultural Society, London. Her awards are numerous and include 'Best of Show' at the National Capitol Orchid Society between 1992–6, a Gold Medal at the RHS show in London, 1995 and an award for Excellence in Botanical Art from the American Society of Botanical Artists in 1998. Her work is held in many private collections and public institutions among which are The Royal Botanic Garden, Kew, The Hunt Institute for Botanical Documentation, Pittsburgh, USA and the Niagara Parks Commission, Niagara Falls, Ontario, Canada. Her published work includes: *The Monograph of the Genus Paphiopedilum*, 2nd edn., Philip Cribb, Royal Botanic Gardens Kew, 1998; *Botanical Illustration in Today's Framework*, D. Bouchier; *The American Gardener Magazine*, Jan/Feb 1998; *Contemporary Botanical Artists, The Shirley Sherwood Collection*, Wiedenfeld and Nicholson 1996; *Curtis's Botanical Magazine*, since 1995; *Orchid Digest* 1995 and *The American Orchid Society Bulletin*, Jan 1998, July 1991.

Fatima Zagonel

Fatima Zagonel was born in Brazil in September 1954 and now lives in Curitiba. She graduated from the Pontificia Universidade Catolica do Parana in 1976 and subsequently graduated in Publicity and Advertising in 1993. In 1977/78/79 she attended courses in art and design in watercolour. She worked as a graphic designer for about twenty years before becoming interested in botanical illustration. Her first contact with botanical illustration was in November 1996 in a workshop presented by Simone Ribeiro and in 1998 she took a course in botanical illustration with Diana Carneiro at the Botanical Museum in Curitiba, supported by the Margaret Mee Foundation in Rio de Janeiro. In May 1999 she received the Margaret Mee Foundation Fellowship, and was instructed by Christabel King at The Royal Botanic Gardens, Kew.

She has been exhibiting her work since 1998 and exhibitions have included the first *Contest Latinoamericano y del Caribe de Ilustration Botanica in Mexico; The Botanical Illustrators of Curitiba* at the Estate Secretary of Commerce in Curitiba; a solo exhibition at the Herbarium of The Royal Botanic Gardens, Kew; and *The Botanical Illustrators of Curitiba* at the Botanical Museum of Curitiba, Brazil. Her work is represented in many private collections including; Mrs Shirley Sherwood, Mrs Ruth Stiff (USA) and The Royal Botanic Gardens, Kew.